A Doctor's Dose
of Inspiration

What a dermatologist learned from
his patients and his life —
wisdom from the skin in.

Volume 1

by Roger T. Moore, MD

Dermwise™

A Doctor's Dose of Inspiration—Volume 1

Dr. Moore's Main Office Location
at time of publication in 2018 is:
DermacenterMD—Elkhart
111 North Nappanee Street
Elkhart, Indiana 46514
(574) 522-0265

www.DermacenterMD.com

ISBN 10: 0-9600631-0-2
ISBN 13: 978-0-9600631-0-9

Cover image iStockphoto

Contents

Acknowledgements

The patients who walk through the doors of our practice are truly special. Each makes me a better person. Our bond is the magic ingredient and inspiration for this book and so much more. Thank you.

A special note of thanks goes to every health care provider and patient who refers others to our team. We are honored and humbled to receive your trust.

As book editor Tammy Barley helped bring these stories to life. She has been a champion and is a true professional.

Last but not least, my wife Amanda has been the anchor of my life, our practice, and our family. She, like many wives and mothers of today, do **so much more** than what is expected of them. She *is* my "**so much more.**"

Introduction

Many years ago a wonderful woman who came into my office told me that every person has a story. She explained that each of us has unique experiences, circumstances, and environmental influences that shape us into who we are.

Over time I have learned what she meant by her comment. We all carry with us moments, struggles, and victories, which all too often remain hidden away inside. Our families, friends, and coworkers never really get to see that part of us.

But something magical takes place when we hear about the struggles and victories of others. It makes people more human and allows us to connect with them on a far deeper level. A bond can be formed, one that can have a lasting impact on our life.

More people than I can count have influenced me through their stories, their actions, and their words. Most of these people will never know that I continue to think of them even years later. The little part of them that has been left with me is something I am humbled and honored to carry forward.

The pages that follow hold just a few of the extraordinary insights from people, books, and life that I have shared in our newsletter over the years. These mini stories remind me that the wonder and power of the human spirit is very much alive and thriving.

I cannot thank each patient enough for being someone who has helped me become just a bit better for the next person who walks through the doors of our office and into my life. It is my sincere hope that as you read the following stories, you will find an invaluable nugget in each that you can carry with you too.

Our journey in life is more than what we take from it. The adventure of everyday living is often the gift we give to others.

We may never know the full results of our efforts. One kind comment, one good deed, or one compassionate moment might be the seedling from which much magnificent fruit grows. So, simply remember that you are unique, truly special, and someone who makes a genuine difference to those in your world.

I wish for you and those you care about all the good that life can bring. At the same time, may you find the opportunity to give and receive the kindness our world should be filled with.

Many happy returns on your good heart, words, and actions.

Enthusiastically,

Roger

Roger Moore, MD

Today's Treasures

Hello, My Friend,

One of our staff happily recounted going back to a high school reunion. It got me to thinking. There are so many people I have met who share personal glory days gone by. Whether reminiscing about high school, college, or even adulthood, each person seems to have a time in the past that was special.

In our office we meet quite a few patients in their eighties. Recently such a woman with a twinkle to her eye said to me, "Oh to be forty again." And a thirty-five-year-old man rekindled his time in college, when he had unlimited energy and strength. The magic of yesteryear seems powerful to many.

When I realized quite a few people talked about their past, it dawned on me that today is tomorrow's past. How many of these people (myself included) had known, during those moments they reminisced about, that those would be the times they would look back on and cherish? This thought also made me wonder if we miss some of the value of this current time in our life, or "the present," because we are too focused on getting through the day.

If we knew that in the future we might look back on today as a wonderful moment in our life, would we view "the present" differently? Would we pause and appreciate the beauty of nature, the dynamics of friendships, the rewarding challenges of work, or the love of family like we should?

Though we may all look back on the best of our lives in some way (that is what memories are for), I would challenge you, and myself too, to act as though the current time in our life is to be cherished. Live as though this is the most abundant and wonderful segment of our existence it can be. If we learn to live in this manner, we just might create a streaming flow of experiences that lead us to a full and magnificent life.

You deserve all the good and wonderful treasures life has to offer. It is up to us to get from the day rather than through the day. Let's take the opportunity to experience most fully the magic of this very moment as we put it into the context of the many days of our life. By thinking of each day as a magnificent gift, we are truly finding the value in "the present."

Road to Hana

If you are like me, you have likely had someone tell you "enjoy the journey." It was a term shared with me various times, but not until it was explained in parable form did it become memorable.

During college an orthopedic surgeon I considered my mentor asked me if I had ever been to Hana. After hearing my reply of no, he went on to share a story.

He said he'd traveled to Hawaii, and several people told him he absolutely had to go to a location on Maui called Hana. So he took a very long road to this destination.

Along the way he saw spectacular waterfalls; a natural, undeveloped shoreline; and the incredible vegetation of Maui's coastal rainforest. Upon arrival at the community of Hana, he felt somewhat let down because, as authentically Hawaiian as the town was, he had expected a magical destination point to exceed his expectations. This did not occur.

This mentor went on to say, in reflecting on the experience, that the beauty of the drive to Hana was in the wonders along the way to his destination. It was not until he arrived at the end of his path that he realized just how magnificent the trip had been.

The beauty was on the road to Hana.

At this point he leaned in, lowered his voice a little, and said, "The trip is like life. The beauty is in the journey. So enjoy where you are at, when you are there."

Through my years in practice, this sentiment has been passed along to me several times by other people as well. Several retired patients have described how the challenges they currently face make them wish they had appreciated their status when they were working.

In day-to-day life—when we are in it—that is where the beauty is. The power of joy lies in finding the meaning and power in each day.

This moment, right now, is the only time we will pass this way. It is up to us to find and make the most of this very day.

May we each learn from the people who have come before us. If we can find a way to see the best in what is given to us now, and enjoy the moments and good things given to us today, we are reaching a stage of enlightenment.

Gold on a Lakeshore

In reading a book by Mark Nero, I found a passage that mirrored some features of my own life, and you might find a few similarities in yours too.

He described being at a large lake on vacation. From his side of the lake, he looked across the calm waters to the other shore. The remote beach area shimmered magnificently, almost exotically, with sunlight and seemed to beckon him. But the distance seemed so far that he wondered if he dare venture to the other side.

On day seven of his vacation, he decided that the next morning he would take his small rowboat and go explore this special beach.

He arose early and made his way across the lake, arriving just as sunrise began. He was a bit taken aback, as the aura of the mysterious was undone. Though the beach he had traveled to see looked generally beautiful and peaceful, the sand was wet and clumpy, just like the beach he had left behind.

He smiled to himself as he looked back across the lake to see, as the sunrise began, that where he had come from shimmered with light on the water, and the beach appeared serene and magical, just like he had seen when looking the opposite direction the previous days. So, he had risen early and traveled to the exotic place, only to find he received a calling to go back to where he had begun.

So often we, and those we know, look for some magic and beauty in the distance, only to find the place we are now is the golden location. Whether it is dreams, work, love, or other desires we have, learning to appreciate who we are, where we are, and who we are with is a lesson worth considering. What we lack may be right here with us, all along.

May you and those you care about appreciate and receive the blessings you deserve in your present location.

Power of a Plant

Quotes from leaders, literary giants, and those with perceived wisdom have been something of interest to me. Though I don't always understand or recognize the intent behind some of them, many have found a way to make an impression on me in one form or another.

Ralph Waldo Emerson was credited with saying, "Use what language you will, you can never say anything but what you are." The author of the book *Personal Development Course* wrote that this quote was a parallel to what he felt was a human law or part of nature's law. He explained that accomplishments can be no greater than the qualities instilled within us.

The author went on to describe how many people look at life as though they are held captive by circumstances. He said that well-meaning people too often fall victim to living with poor relationships and/or tough social or work situations, without looking to change the one thing they have the most control over: *oneself.*

The point he taught was that our best avenue toward a better life is to learn how to improve ourselves.

Self-improvement is not always about choosing the better or easier way. Nor is it about avoiding pain or heartbreak. Self-improvement means growing from the circumstances we encounter, all the while expanding who we are and what we can handle going forward.

Intentional self-growth is a powerful skill which too few use. The mindset (and quote) to "grow where you're planted" enables us become the best version of ourselves.

Though no one wishes for problems, if we can find a way to grow stronger and better with the next hurdle or roadblock in life, we will be expanding who we are. And that can happen when we ask ourselves, *How can I learn from this situation to become a better person?*

Then we and those we care about will benefit from the growth gained through life's challenges.

"I Dare You"

If you have ever been told these words, "I dare you," you are not alone. One author even used these words as a title for his book. "Who was this guy," you may wonder, "and what does it have to do with me?" Let's explore.

William Danforth wrote a book with the crazy title of *I Dare You*. In his writings he drives home the point that we each have challenges in life, and it is not until we respond to these with confidence and grit that we discover the person we are capable of becoming.

Even one of our most famous presidents, Abe Lincoln, lived a life packed with challenges and uphill battles. Time after time he had to overcome defeat. That attitude of resiliency, never give up, and always do your best resonates throughout Mr. Danforth's book.

He believes many in the world live with unused talents and latent ability. It is through catching a glimpse of your own abilities by pressing forward a little more and a little more, and the art of encouraging others to similarly reach their potential, that you broaden your horizon.

How did this help William Danforth? Well, he worked to unleash his abilities and had a passion for helping others find their potential. He used this in the business world until he grew his company to become known by most every person who has ever owned a dog, cat, horse, or zebra. William Danforth was known as the man who founded Ralston Purina company, a world leader in providing food for animals, among other ventures. He used his philosophies to teach his employees and required many of them to read his book *I dare you.*

Finding your hidden potential, by pushing forward more and more, can unleash a side of you that lights up your talents and expands the capacities for growth in you and those around you. It is akin to finding gold in the mountain right outside your door.

You possess a wealth you might not know exists. Whatever you do in life, I encourage you to continually expand your horizons a bit further than you think you can. You might find a wonderful world waiting for you and break through the chains that may have limited you.

At the same time, encouraging those you care about can help them discover more inside of them than they knew was present.

"I dare you" to be a bit more today than you were yesterday!

From Rusted Cars to Butterflies

A gentleman recently shared with me a bit about his pastime. He collected cars, not the most fancy, he said, but when he found a good deal, he would take advantage of it. One of his cars was a 1978 Thunderbird with only 17,000 miles on it.

He said that none of his cars was overly valuable, and that he didn't put a great deal of money into these cars like some people do. He simply enjoyed finding a good deal on a vehicle, and then working to make it look and run well. From there he maintained the cars to keep them in excellent shape.

When he mentioned that he had ten vehicles, I wondered what it took to keep them in excellent shape. I'd been taught that a vehicle has to be driven, at least some of the time, or malfunctions start occurring. Being the person who frequently ties analogies to my own life, I couldn't help but think that if my skills were hinges, many would be rusted.

Like cars, we need to continually use our skills and find ways to improve what we have so they don't wither away . . . and so they can benefit other people.

As a child in school, I was once so terrified to speak in front of a class that I actually felt ill, to the point I stayed home from school that day. As an adult I've been thrust into the role of public speaker due to my chosen career, and have somehow found a way to speak before an audience when required. Now, that does not mean I don't get a swarm of butterflies in my stomach, but it does mean through educating myself on the topic, and practice, that somehow the butterflies fly in formation a little more often these days.

May we all find a way to realize, more and more, the vast wealth of skills we each have. Many of us are endowed with gifts just waiting to be rekindled or used. I wish you and those you care about a full realization of who you can be!

Buoyancy amid Changing Tides

Someone once told me that ships can provide insight into how to handle life's challenges. Though I have never been on a large ship, I am amazed at their engineering and ability to stay afloat.

When a ship is placed in the water, gravity pulls it down. At the same time, the water that is displaced by the ship pushes upward with a constant force on the ship, termed buoyant force.

The science of this is described by Archimedes' Principle (where the buoyant force is equal to the weight of the displaced fluid). Though a bit confusing to me at first, an Internet search helped me understand that a large hull of a ship, shaped in the proper manner, can support a great deal of weight, if it pushes away enough water.

Regardless of the level of water around it, a well-designed ship will stay at the surface of the water. This simple phenomenon is something we as people could take note of for our own lives. At times the pressures of the world bear against us, challenge us, or toss us about, in what seem insurmountable ways. Other times the nuances of situations or people around drag us down.

The strength of ships and people sometimes lies in the ability to remain stable, hold steady, and know we are built to withstand the pressures of the environment. No matter what is happening below a ship, it will rise above it. No matter what pressures attempt to force it down, it has the strength to bear up. So, when faced with unexpected challenges, we should remind ourselves that we can rise with the tides of our life. Being firm, steady, and stable can help us navigate the storms we face.

May we each find strength, like a well-designed ship, to stay above the situations that try to drag us down and rise above the pressures in our life. May we also handle each day with unbending resolve. Lastly, like ships returning to port, we should remember to spend time recharging, emotionally and spiritually.

Know that you are strong, powerful, and wise in a way that deserves success in life's ventures.

Triumph Glue

Today, we often hear stories about children acting out, politicians acting inappropriately, and famous people doing silly things. It seems like the world lacks discipline. Discipline for doing wrong? Maybe. But maybe something else entirely is needed. How about a commitment to do right?

If there is a critical ingredient to success in life, that ingredient is discipline. One small word, rejected by so many, yet it plays such a vital role in happiness, relationships, money, and achievement. Specifically, *self*-discipline.

Most people envision failure as one major event, such as bankruptcy, divorce, or a car accident. However, failure is rarely one event. Most often it is a culmination of many small errors in judgement, usually due to lack of self-discipline.

Curiously, people tend not to realize there is a glue that binds success to effort. This ingredient, self-discipline, is the irreplaceable foundation for success. The lack of it ultimately leads to failure.

Learning to be aware of our small decisions today can lead to becoming dramatically more successful in the future. A goal to lose weight or become healthier is only attained with daily decisions. Choosing to eat well today or exercise today, each and every day, will lead to resounding success, and triumph, but it takes time—and self-discipline.

We should start the process of improvement today, even if it means we start small. Then continue the same commitment every day. Remember, it is the culmination of small decisions and self-discipline, compounded over time, that leads to positive results.

There is no better way and no better person who deserves the many rewards of self-discipline than the person reading this right now. May you find the resounding success you deserve with your daily beneficial choices.

Baseball Wisdom

Sports figures are not often given credit for their intellectual prowess. During an interview, Chicago Cubs manager Joe Maddon made comments I consider quite wise.

In the preceding April 2018 game, Javier Baez of the Cubs flipped his bat in a manner the Pittsburgh Pirate manager took exception to. Sometime after the game, the Pirate's skipper criticized Baez for "not respecting the game." Interestingly, the player had already been told by his own teammates that his actions did not look the best and reflect the type of person he is. He quickly apologized to his teammates, coaches, and others. The criticism from the opponent came after the player had already been told of his wrong, accepted responsibility, and apologized. Baez mentioned how he did not want children watching to get the wrong impression.

Joe Maddon, the Cubs manager, commented on the situation during his interview, after he learned of the opposing manager's criticism of his player. He said, "Most of the time when you hear critical commentary, it's really, pretty much, self-evaluation. It's about what you believe, it's about your judgmental component. It reveals *you* more than it reveals the person you're talking about."

He went on to remind us that when we want to be hypercritical of someone, it is best to understand we are revealing ourselves and what we believe. It shows the type of person and character the criticizer is.

After I read his comments, I had to go back and reread them. What a powerful statement he made. I could not help but remember my own father who was slow to criticize others in public and fast to give praise. Though my father was demanding, expected things done right, and expected the best effort, in public he was rarely critical of anyone.

From Joe Maddon and my late father, I find a reminder to be cautious with criticism. Consider how things can be said in a private manner, and also in a way to help rather than deteriorate a situation or relationship.

The good-seekers, and those who share good with others around them, tend to be like magnets. They create bonds, uplift others, and make people feel good about themselves.

If only this concept were understood and practiced by the majority of the world's people. The good done today and going forward is what builds, and helps form, the future of the next generation.

If each person embarked on their day looking for the best in others, that feeling of belief and confidence would spread from one person to another. The end result might very well be that we each live in a brighter, more positive environment.

May you reap the rewards of your good deeds and wise, uplifting words.

Masons and Cathedrals

A kind person shared with me how uncomfortable the feeling usually was when he went to the hospital for an urgent medical condition. The culmination of fear was almost unbearable.

What happened next reminded me of a story Cavett Robert shared in one of his books. He described two masons at work during the heat of the day, placing bricks and mortar along a wall. A passerby stopped and asked them what they were doing. One wiped the sweat from his brow, let out a sigh, and said he was being paid—full pay for the shift and double time after five in the afternoon—to lay one brick at a time.

The second man looked up, smiled, and stated, "I am building a cathedral, one that will be a cornerstone of my community for generations to come."

The reason this story came to mind was that our patient said one of the hospital volunteers, termed a redcoat, had recently taken the time to walk him to the proper location for registration, made sure he had something to write with, and then asked if anything else was needed. Before the volunteer left, he gave his name and told him if he could help in any way going forward to let him know.

The anxiety of our patient was greatly reduced, and he appreciated the effort which he viewed as nothing short of a gift he had been given.

The volunteer's impact reminded me of the mason who had the grand vision for the work he was doing. The patient experience was incredibly positive due to an effort and level of care that resonated with him during his time of need. In pondering the two scenarios, I wondered if we realized how much our role in the lives of those we contact actually plays. Do we understand that the interactions we have each day could improve quality of life for those around us?

If we looked at our interactions with others as a small piece of something bigger for each person we connected with, would we act differently? We never know when a kind word, a pleasant gesture, or a willing ear to listen could really matter in a way that the future of another person might be altered.

Take the opportunity to do something kind for another person each day this week, and you may very well help build something grand, which can last longer than you know.

Farmer Unflappable

I read a story about a fellow who stopped for breakfast at a diner where the waitress beamed with happiness. As he sat down, she said to him, "It's a wonderful day, isn't it?"

His reply was that of a grumpy Gus as he retorted, "What's so good about this day anyway?"

Without missing a beat, she replied, "If it's not that good of a day, try missing one, and you would find out."

The small exchange reminded me how precious each day really is. We walk through this life just one time. We get the chance to make best of today and every day only once.

I am far from one to teach about demeanor since there have been way too many of my days spent worrying, stewing, grumpy, or otherwise not displaying my best for myself and those around me. Yet I can't help but think about how calm and unflappable my grandfather, a farmer, had always seemed to be. He probably realized at some point that one negative event does not make a day bad. He also refused to let one bad day extend itself over into the next. At the same time, he seemed to look for and find the best in the people around him.

When I worked the farm with my grandfather in my youth, I observed that there seemed to always be something wrong, broken, or needing to be fixed. Many of the problems we had to fix came from my direct actions. I can remember breaking off fence posts, getting tractors stuck, and running my tractor out of diesel way out in the field, just to name a few. Though I might have felt like a total fool for some of the mistakes I made, my grandfather never called me stupid. Instead he had a way of making me feel that problems or mistakes were easy to fix. Somehow he met challenges with a smile and made those around him glad to be in his presence.

The people who look for the best in the people and situations around them tend to be those I want to be around. If we think about the fact that like attracts like, then we might find ourselves better off maintaining a demeanor we want to present to the world, in hopes it gets reflected back in the type of people and attitudes around us.

In my experience, it often does.

Lincoln's Insight

How do you respond to bad news, a difficult person, or a disappointment? If you are like most of us, patterns have developed that function like autopilot—they go into motion when things are off-kilter in your world. This is not always the necessary response.

The way we deal with challenging situations is a habit we developed over time, a habit that may not serve us well. We might overreact, blow things out of proportion, or worry more than a specific problem is worth. Over time the reaction we bring forth becomes a reflex. It is often disproportionate to the issue at hand.

When we take a step back and analyze ourselves, we might even find our reactions immobilize us or hurt those near us. The response is often counterproductive to the result we truly want.

If instead we simply pause, and take inventory of the situation, we might realize the particular problem is worth a more measured response. There is no need to harm another person's feelings with an outburst, an angry look or gesture, or damage our own reputation through our actions.

Recognizing a response pattern is the first step in learning to handle situations in a more positive and effective way.

Remind yourself that the minutes and hours spent worked up over most problems are rarely worth the effort we put in to them. Abraham Lincoln once stated, "I worried about a lot of things in life and *some* of them actually happened." His observation was a wise one.

So the next opportunity we have to get worked up, let us remember to pause and recall that few situations benefit from or warrant overreaction, but instead a more measured, thought-out response. You will feel better, and those around you will likely appreciate the new you.

The Dairyman

If you ever wonder where all of the good people are, know that they are living right here as our acquaintances and neighbors.

A former dairyman, who raised a wonderful family, finds a way to brighten the day of our team every time he comes into the office. His smile and pleasant demeanor leave a wake of warm and happy feelings behind him. Though he's had challenges with his skin, including skin cancer, he finds a way to enhance the day of those he encounters during each visit.

It's not often people realize how important their own attitude is to those who care for them. The fact that this gentleman makes a point to greet each medical assistant with a smile and ask them how they are makes them feel that they matter to him. His caring way causes those around him want to help him even more.

He reminds me of an author who stated there is a law of reciprocity: how we treat others will be returned to us in kind. Now, it might not always turn out the way we want, but we can consider others in our actions.

In doing so we may very well make our own environment happier and more peaceful. If we understand our own personal world is one that we have control over, then why not make it the most delightful place to be?

Who doesn't want people to smile and give them a handshake or hug when they arrive? Often it is the person who makes others feel welcome with their words and actions who is greeted most warmly.

I must admit, there are many times I have sat on the sidelines and wondered what makes a person seem to have such ease with others. The truth may very well be that they don't have ease, as much as they are willing to be first in acting how they want others to act toward them.

They invoke the law of reciprocity.

In our future, may we plant seeds of goodness, knowing that in time the harvest will be one we are glad to be part of.

Greatest Discovery

Have you ever stopped to think about how much control we have of our own attitudes?

We see a lot of people in our office, and I find it amazing how many have truly positive outlooks.

A perfect example was when I walked into an exam room one day and encountered a walker placed beside a middle-aged woman with a beaming smile. As I talked with her, she shared that she had been in a terrible car accident since we last saw her, causing her a great deal of pain and continual physical therapy as well as a walker to facilitate getting around.

She explained her recovery briefly and then quickly shifted to how grateful she was for her remaining health and the opportunity to spend more time with her grandchildren, whom she obviously adored. She was so appreciative of the opportunities she had for that day and going forward that I was amazed. Her genuine smile and sparkling eyes brightened the room.

William James was a physician who offered what many believe was the first course in psychology in the United States. He once said, "The greatest discovery of my generation is that a human can alter his life by altering his attitude."

Though this woman was in the thralls of physical therapy and had every right to be resentful, she found a way to focus on what was left, not what was lost. Her resilience and attitude were not only inspiring to me, but also most likely set a wonderful example for those grandchildren she cherished so much.

No one person makes it through life without struggles and disappointments. If in any way we can muster the wherewithal to find the positive turn in the circumstances we are dealt, we might very well be the beacon of light that inspires someone else.

As we do so, may the world reflect back the optimism and encouragement we need to carry forward.

This Is Possible

Sometimes it seems like people have an easy life. The appearance may not fit what has actually occurred, though. This was quite the case for a retired pediatric dentist whom our office is fortunate to care for.

This man retired to live out his life on a lake, but in learning about his past, to suggest he would become a dentist at all, let alone retire, would seem beyond improbable. Why? His life hurdles were amazing.

At the age of eight, while in France, his father left his family behind so he could search for better opportunities in the United States. Shortly after leaving, his father learned his wife was pregnant, so he sent for her to ensure the new child would be born in the United States. Our patient and his sister were left behind at separate relatives' homes because the father could not afford to send for them at that time.

It took years before his father scraped together enough money to send for our patient and his sister. After arriving in the U.S. and then graduating high school, he began work in the factory with his father. He subsequently obtained a job in a dental lab, due to his metal-working skills learned in the factory. His work in the dental lab was such high quality that an orthodontist hired him. After years in this role, and with a family, he was fairly content with his path in life.

It was only through the encouragement of his boss, the orthodontist, that he decided to complete his college prerequisites and afterward apply to dental school. So he went to college at night while working his full-time job. In time, he attained admission to a dental school.

His prior employer helped finance some of the college prerequisites, and he worked extra hours in the summers, utilizing his expertise in metal working, to help start the orthodontic educational aspect for his dental school (all this while supporting his family and raising kids).

His life story is certainly not done justice by the small amount I have shared. However, his comments that "America is the greatest country in the world, where someone like me can through hard work, attain a degree, and afford to retire is amazing" displays some of his attitude.

He shared with me that the land of opportunity is still the U.S.

In my own humble view, I would say his life is a series of steps, where he continued to progress forward regardless of the hurdles put in front of him. He shows what can be accomplished from meager beginnings and persistence.

Though most people may not become dentists, the opportunity to make the world a better place through attitude, encouragement, and perseverance are possible for most of us. May you and those you care about find some of the magic and goodness this gentleman shared, so that you have, at the very least, a wonderful outlook on life.

Billions, with a "B"

Counting the number of our failures isn't always healthy. Or, *is* it?

If you're like me, there's a little voice in your head that creeps up when you feel like you haven't performed at your best. Whether it follows a setback, a goof-up, or simply a deficiency while trying to meet your own expectations, that voice sneaks right in. Confidence can be destroyed really quick.

While reading an article in *USA Today* about the founder of Spanx, a women's undergarment, the failure concept was described in a different way, one that resonated with and enlightened me.

She said that once each week, at dinner, her father invited her and her siblings to share what they had failed at during the previous days. The atmosphere was one in which setbacks were expected. They meant a person was striving to achieve their goals.

She went on to describe how learning to fail helped her on a path of success she could only have achieved through handling setbacks. The number of times her clothing concept was shot down were many, as were the number of manufacturers who declined to make her product, and then the challenges of sales. Too many to count.

Through her father's teaching, she had learned that failure was not final. Her persistence, determination, and a bit of luck rocketed her company to success . . . and landed her as a billionaire.

Though few people will achieve the financial success of this woman, I have to ask, if you are like me, could we live a bit better each day, if we changed the tune of that little voice in our heads?

If, after a setback, the thought creeps in that we are inferior, could we tell ourselves, "This is good, because I'm advancing toward my goals, and I will learn and grow from this experience"? If so, we might find good amid life's troubles.

The setbacks might become stepping-stones to a better version of who we are.

As you pass through your tomorrows, I hope, if that little voice in your head talks like mine, you can change the words so that they embrace a better version of you. You deserve abundant success, peace, and happiness.

Habits for Humanity

You may or may not have heard about former President Jimmy Carter being diagnosed with the deadly skin cancer, melanoma. This was revealed publicly in August 2015. He cut short his trip to Guyana earlier in the year (May) because he wasn't feeling well. After being evaluated he was found to have a mass on his liver.

The mass was surgically removed. Unfortunately he was found soon after to have masses in the brain, which means the disease has likely spread, and is thus termed metastatic cancer.

As famous as he has become, more so after his presidency ended, it is sad to think of this disease affecting him or any human. Though it may not be the case for President Carter, most melanomas arise in the skin, which is why we encourage each person to look at their skin every month and come in for a full skin exam at our office each year. Melanoma can be easily treated when it is caught early. However, when it is not caught early, melanoma can become life threatening.

In looking at President Carter, it is fascinating to realize he has ties to so many people around the world. In the community of our practice, we even have several patients who have met him personally. One couple grew close to President and Mrs. Carter through their many years of wintering in Georgia and volunteering with the Carters' efforts in Habitat for Humanity. One other gentleman before he passed away actually loaned the services of his company's corporate jet to have Mrs. Carter fly to Michigan to visit a friend's son in need of her counseling. Yet another couple told me they had spent time in the Sunday school class President Carter taught in Georgia.

Quite amazing how one former president can have a reach into our community. At the same time, he likely has a similar reach into many communities. When we stop and think about the connection, it is not the presidency that created this bond. It is the drive President Carter has had to give back and help the less privileged of the world that has drawn people to him.

And when we look at this situation from another angle, we can see that everyone needs to be like-minded in order to facilitate building such bonds. It is nice to think so many of our country's wonderful communities are built of people like President Carter, who want to make the world a better place.

I know each of us would wish only all the best for anyone who fights through the changes of melanoma. It would be nice to take notice of the fact President Carter's influence grew greater when he helped those in need than even when he was president.

If each person gives just a bit each day to make the world better, the collective effort of all will make a resounding difference.

Hospital Dedication

A wonderful man shared his hospital experience with me that made me realize how powerful a helping hand can be.

This ninety-two-year-old man came in for his routine visit. He told me he'd recently been admitted to the hospital for pneumonia. For four days in the hospital, he barely ate or drank because he had developed painful sores inside his mouth. His sugars (blood glucose) had bounced up dramatically above normal, staying near 500 for some time. He was exhausted, wasting away, and felt like he couldn't get any better.

No one on the hospital health care team had answers as to why this was occurring.

On Saturday morning a nurse walked in the room. Believing he was ready to go (meaning he was ready to give up on this life), he waved at her and moaned, "Go on, get out of here." The nurse ignored his plea. She told him she was there for him, and "we" would get through this.

She brought a suction apparatus, like dentists use, and sat down beside him, refusing to leave. For the next four hours, she would take a moist sponge with a handle on it, dab the sponge around the inside of his mouth, and then instruct him to suction the area. By lunchtime the wounds were crusting and white material was removed.

At the end of four hours, he was able to eat and drink for the first time in days. His recovery was so quick after this that he was able to go home the next day.

He said, "My angel nurse stuck by me and resolved we would make it through. She stayed right by my side. She never left."

I can't explain the depth of feelings emanating from him as he looked me in the eye and shared his experience. I still feel a bit overwhelmed by the dedication of this nurse and his rapid recovery. Whether she realizes it or not, she was his angel and will always be thought of this way.

I have to think that we all may be able to help another person, in some form. We simply never know how close that person is to giving up, maybe not on life, but on believing in him- or herself.

A kind word or deed might encourage someone on during their time of need.

If we all share a bit of the good we have inside with those around us, more people will be able to find the success they deserve.

I wish you all the best as you strive to make a kind and caring difference in the lives of others.

Steel Steps

A simple concept applied repeatedly can yield a significant return on investment. Now what in the world could this mean? I will tell you, at least from the perspective of a patient who revealed it to me.

When I asked about his career, this former president of a steel-processing company said he and his brother had founded the business in 1984. Basically, they took steel in coils from steel mills and made it into manufacturer-ready products for customers.

The two brothers grew the business to more than one hundred employees. It played a significant role in the local economy, not to mention the lives of those he worked with. He operated with integrity and strong values, like he lived his life.

A fundamental concept the two brothers held and asked of every co-worker was this: "Let's be a little bit better today than we were yesterday."

While discussing this concept of getting better each day, this man's passion for quality, care of others, and doing the best possible job was evident.

As a leader he was able to get a whole organization to move in a positive direction and improve each day. The concept, multiplied over many days, months, and years, led the organization to resounding success. He explained that this concept helped propel them forward to a level they could not have imagined.

And after thirty years in business, he and his brother built a significant company, which they were able to sell and retire from in 2014.

In thinking about his concept, I became fascinated with the thought of this being practiced daily for three decades. If every person in whatever endeavor they participate in (parenting, work, social activities, faith practices, or other) could make each day a step forward, then the improvement over time could be incredible. What heights one would reach!

Some people I meet want results in a few months and seem to quit trying if they aren't where they had hoped in a year. If only they could use this man's mindset of the long view! Think about the improvements one could make with consistent application of this principle for five or ten years. The long view, meshed with dedication to daily self-improvement, could produce extremely advantageous results for many.

May you and those you love find the success you desire along the many-years journey ahead.

Achieving Harmony

A wonderful couple came into the office for an appointment. While we chatted for a few minutes, they mentioned they do marriage counseling as part of their retirement activities. The passion and enthusiasm for this work was evident in the wife's radiant face as she described what they did.

I found this a different method of spending time together than what I typically hear and asked to learn a bit more.

The husband and wife beamed as they sat in the exam room side by side. It was the type of glow that people who are content and at peace seem to share with the world around them. If I remember correctly, the wife said they had been married for thirty-seven years. Then she followed up with a statement that twenty-seven of those were the most wonderful of their lives . . . and the first ten were the years that made it possible for them to be marriage counselors.

She said they were able to give others insights now because they had learned them from working through their own challenges over the years. Eventually they had found peace together.

Their own life experiences helped them relate to those who had problems, since they had likely been there too. Together they believed their calling at this point in life was helping others to find harmony in their marital relationships.

After meeting this amazing couple, I began to think of marriage as being similar to two people being tied together by a long string. If both people go their own way, eventually the slack in the string is out and a tug will stop the progress of each individual who is heading their own direction. However, if the two work together, they travel together in most any direction they want with harmony and less tension.

The retired husband and wife were helping married people reduce the tension between them, teaching them to move through life in a more connected and congruent way.

May we each realize, like this couple did, that the times of tension in life can be followed by harmony if we look to see how we can best work with others.

Whether a business partnership, a parent/child relationship, or marriage, working together can bring infinitely more positive outcomes than the alternative. May you find the harmony in your life and experience the glow and happiness it brings.

Acorn of Significance

Have you ever pondered how magical, mystical, and complex the world of nature truly is? Thinking of all the minor and major requirements for just one blade of grass, flower, or tree to grow boggles the mind.

Just consider—an acorn falls from an oak tree. It lies on the ground. When, and only when, its environment supports growth, the acorn will start to change to become a seedling. From there, it can develop into a wonderful and robust oak tree.

Now, considering humans is even more incredible. The components and intricate balance of air, water, nutrients, sunshine, and rest needed to sustain our lives is downright fascinating. Yet you and I also have personalities, the influences of others, and life events that shape each of us into the unique individuals we are. We are so much more complex than the nature that surrounds us.

In fact, each human being is so distinctive, genetically and by their own lived experiences, that no two are the same. Every person is special.

We are each someone whose life has brought him or her to this moment in time. Together we are here, and yet we each bring our own views and interpretations.

We can stand in a crowd with similarities and yet also be fantastically unalike.

And, perhaps most significant of all, each of us and those we meet today have experienced and overcome so much to be who we are at this very moment.

Remember that you are stronger than an oak tree, more unique than you can imagine, and truly special to those around you. May you find joy and beauty in yourself and in those you meet today. The world is a special place, in large part due to who you are.

The Extraordinary Ordinary

Do you know how you hear a comment, it sticks in your mind, and then you wonder why it's there? Then you are like me. At times, other people's simple words or actions float back into my thoughts, and then some time later I find meaning in them.

I often ask people if they've been up to anything exciting or fun recently. The answers to the question are so varied that it shows me how different—and how alike—we all are. I love to learn through the experiences of others.

On one visit a wonderful woman I had seen for years responded to my question with, "I am an appreciator of the ordinary." She explained that she didn't define her time between our visits by any grand trip or experiences but rather by enjoying the common and repetitive moments she encountered each day.

Her sentiment "appreciator of the ordinary" had come back to me now and then, though it was not until I read a passage from a book that I realized what she'd meant.

The book's author described how life provides us with difficulties and disappointments, as well as victories and times of happiness. It is when we accept life for what it is, and what it brings to us, that we can find peace and value in the present moment. The author described how magnificence and the extraordinary are often waiting quietly beneath that which we initially consider "ordinary."

The broken glass and the diamond can both reflect a sparkling ray of light. The stroke of a guitar and the dripping of rain can both create musical sounds we can appreciate. Whether we're on our porch or atop a mountain, the world has beauty and wonder waiting to be recognized. It is when we appreciate the magnificence of the "ordinary" that we find the life we are living is the one we are meant to be in.

The beauties of the world are all around us, and more importantly, they are within us. It is up to us to savor them. May we each find something in the daily life we live that reminds us of the wonders of our world.

The lamp's purpose in guiding our path may not be to shine brightness, but to provide enlightenment. To this point, may we each find the value in this woman's wise words and appreciate what is our "ordinary."

Airports, Coffee, and Changing the World

Isn't it uplifting to meet people who are friendly?

While on vacation, my daughter and I stood in line at a coffee shop in the Minneapolis airport. The man behind us said, "That's quite a colorful outfit there, young lady." My daughter wore brightly colored pants and had a striped backpack. We both turned to find a man in his sixties with gray hair, warm eyes, and a smile as wide as could be. "I have five children," he added, "obviously older than you now. But I'm sure a few of my daughters would love your outfit."

Now my daughter is a bit shy, but this introduction and kind comment just caused her to glow. She smiled back at the friendly man, and a conversation ensued.

This interaction got me to thinking. Almost every day we have opportunities to interact with new people, and the world seems to need a few more friendly faces. A few more people who interact with others and make them feel good about themselves.

You see, it didn't cost that man any money or extra time, but it created in my daughter and myself a memory together that will likely last a lifetime. I'm not saying we should each try and make everlasting comments to people we don't even know. Rather, we could easily say something kind, interact with others in a positive way, or simply smile. Any of those can help uplift someone else.

In the old days of small-town America, according to many seniors, everyone knew each other and spoke every time they saw one another. It's amazing to me how, even today, some folks seem to have that same aura about them wherever they go. They are often the ones engaging the cashier, the barista at the coffee shop, or reaching out to those around them. They are creating an uplifting world for themselves and others by their actions.

Most of us want the world to be a better place. Though we may not realize it, we are often the responsible party for the world and environment in which we live. We can make the world better, at least our corner of it, by being the warmth and friendliness we want to see.

The next time you are in the store, with friends, or at a social gathering, engage a bit more with other people around you. It may help uplift you, and it most likely will add sunshine to their day. You might also be surprised at the returns on your good deeds.

Apple of Insight

Seeing things from another person's point of view allows us to gain insight. This was wonderfully displayed by second graders sitting at a lunch table.

One of our patients, who works for the Indiana State Police, took the day off to have lunch with her second-grade son. She sat down at the lunchroom table in a seat too small for an adult, but just right for a caring parent. With her knees folded up high, she listened in on the second graders' conversations.

It was all fun and games, until a serious concern was raised by one young girl. She said she had a loose tooth and knew it was going to fall out soon. Her parents had packed an apple in her lunch. She expressed to the table of children her fear that if she dared to eat the apple, she might lose her tooth in it. She was truly concerned and afraid that she would not have a tooth to put under her pillow for the Tooth Fairy.

The parent didn't barge in, but rather watched closely as the second graders gave careful thought to this problem, then volleyed ideas around the table, as the situation could be one they might very well have in the future.

Then the parent's son said to the girl, "If you *do* lose it in the apple, why don't you just put the apple under your pillow?"

Problem solved. The whole group sighed with relief, and she proceeded to eat her apple.

This scenario serves a reminder that each person carries with them their own challenges, specific to that person, their age, and their stage in life. No matter what their problems are, they are as real and serious to that person as they can be.

If we can find a way to sit quietly and listen to other's burdens, we might see things from their point of view, and we might begin to understand them more fully. Then we would be better equipped to contribute more meaningful solutions.

As we listen with an attentive ear, we might find and endear harmony in the world around us. And we might just learn something valuable ourselves.

BB Humor

Life is fun and entertaining. It is up to us to find the humor in it at times. In some instances we have others who kindly share their life experiences to add levity to our life. One of our patients, at the age of ninety-three, shared a story of his youth that reminded him and me, in a way that had us both chuckling, that what comes around goes around.

Like most children of his generation, he had a BB gun that he could shoot objects with, to hone his skills. The days he described were before television, when skipping rocks, riding horses, and firing BB guns were pastimes for kids.

When he was a boy, his family had a chicken coup with a little door on the side, just the right size for a chicken. On one particular day, this gentleman had felt a bit ornery and, after toting around his BB gun, saw an opportunity to "goose," or incentivize, a chicken that was heading into the small hen house through the door.

Though quite a distance away, he unleashed the perfect shot. *Right on target!* he thought. The chicken cackled and feathers flew as the bird hopped swiftly through the door without looking back.

To be clear, he was not intending to harm the chicken since he did not want to meet the wrath of his parents. He was simply having farm-boy fun at the expense of the poor chicken.

He went on to describe how, that very same week, his mother cooked eggs for a meal. When he bit down, something was too hard to break. Low and behold, it was a BB. Now he had to explain to the family how the BB had gotten into his egg.

I could only imagine how the BB had gotten into the egg his mother had cooked for him, but I sure enjoyed the smile and twinkle in his eye as this kind man shared a humorous event that took place some eighty-five years ago.

In his case he'd had to eat what he had shot, and he'd had to explain himself. In addition to being cautious with a BB gun, his story reminds us we sometimes reap what we sow, even as children.

May you find bits of humor in your day, even if it's reliving childhood antics that bring a chuckle. It can help yourself and those around you, since laughter burns calories, relieves stress, and helps heal, according to several medical studies. I wish you fun and joy!

Goat Gains

At times we learn the most important insights when they come to us from the eyes of a child.

One of our wonderful patients wrote a book about her life. At one point, she wrote, she gave up her work as a physician's assistant to follow a passion she had developed for raising goats.

A friend had brought her six-year-old daughter to visit the farm, and the girl eagerly pitched in to help out. She lugged a bundle of hay over to feed to the goats, happy all the while. As she tugged and dragged the hay, she said, "Raising goats is fun."

Now, the average person would look at what the child was doing and label it "work." To her, it was sheer joy.

The difference between her and someone else who might complain or groan doing the same task was one of perspective. Her outlook helped determine her disposition. And ultimately, it determined her experience that day.

In reading the passage, I couldn't help but feel remorse as my thoughts reflected on times I had been with family and coworkers and let my disposition be negative. My own grumpiness or agitation made not only my day less than optimal, but worse yet, it damaged the day of the people I cared about.

If the perspective of a child could be implemented more often, many of the nuances of life could go more smoothly. We might find joy in tasks considered work, find peace in traversing obstacles, and appreciate the events of the day more often.

May we each consider the viewpoint of a child more routinely, and then experience the joy that comes with it.

This Generous

The heart of a child can reveal itself in the purest manner while brightening the world around it. This becomes evident when a child gets the chance to speak what they are thinking. One such instance showed me just how caring one young patient truly was.

This shy six-year-old boy had a skin problem significant enough he has been to our office on several occasions. On this visit, a biopsy was required. The boy remained very polite though not too talkative throughout the procedure. During my conversation with him, I let him know that I admired his cowboy boots. They were like a pair I once owned when I was young. I attempted to break through the ice by offering to trade him my black dress shoes for his pair of boots.

He politely declined and said that his boots would not likely fit me. He smiled, perhaps at the thought of me trying to fit my big feet into his little boots. Or maybe he was thinking about how silly it would be to return to school in the boat-sized shoes of his dermatologist.

He continued to stay rather quiet, even while his mother and I wrapped things up. At the end of his visit, I said a warm good-bye and left the room.

Later that day, one of the medical assistants told me that, after I had left the room, the young boy said to his mother, "Maybe if I save my allowance, I could buy him a pair of boots."

The thought that this six-year-old, with his ongoing medical problem, was willing to even consider using his allowance to show me a kindness still gives me a heavy heart. What a caring young boy he is. How amazing his parents must be to be raising a child who thinks like this. His thoughts and actions still leave me speechless.

In thinking back about how wonderful this young boy is, I can't help but think how magnificent this world truly must be when people like him are in line to be the next generation of leaders. This type of thinking and caring is what will lift our society to a brighter future. The tomorrows have to be bright when six-year-olds are so generous, thoughtful, and kind.

May we each bring value to our future by caring, sharing, and helping along the younger generation in some way. The time we spend is an investment in the most well-deserving.

A Salute to Moms

If you have children, you know the relationship you have with them is invaluable. The wonders of children are often the power that fuels many parents' lives.

My wife and I have three children. The two youngest are girls. As the kids have grown older, I have watched them bond with my wife in an unwavering manner. Seeing the beauty of this relationship, I find pride and contentment to know they are in good and loving hands.

To be totally frank, though, I long for that attachment at times. Now, some will say girls need their moms, and boys do too, for that matter. There is something magical about a mother's touch, her willingness to listen without passing judgment, and her heart, which is always guiding toward good.

In looking at our three children, I realize one of the special components I see is my wife's positive impact on who they have become. One of the greatest features is her continual willingness to serve the children. She provides rides to events, makes sure each is dressed just right, and makes herself available when called upon.

It was written in a very important book (aka the Bible) something to the effect that the greatest among us will be the one who serves others. This model of servant leadership is no better exemplified in most families than through the words and actions of the mother, which children observe and eventually emulate.

If you were fortunate enough to have had a mother who helped you, have a wonderful wife who made the lives of your children better, or if you simply know or see a mother making a difference in her child's life, I encourage you to tell her *thank you* today. Too many times moms are not recognized for all the sacrifices they make to ensure the life of the family goes well. A bit of recognition, acknowledgment, and appreciation is long overdue for most moms.

May you find rewards for the good deeds you have done, and may one of those be thanking a mother. Your action may help a mother who needs that bit of encouragement right now.

In this spirit, thank you to every mother.

Influence of a Twelve-Year-Old Poet

Not long ago a quote from the famous English poet William Henley caught my eye. The quote read, "I am the master of my fate, I am the captain of my soul." The words, when pondered, can have a different meaning for each of us, because we can likely apply them to where we are at this very moment.

The quote is actually the two closing lines of Mr. Henley's 1875 poem, which was originally unnamed but later given the title *Invictus*, Latin for *unconquered*.

It has been said that he wrote the poem during his early battle with tuberculosis, which he contracted at the age of twelve. The disease infected his bones, requiring an amputation of the left leg below the knee. Despite this setback, and later spending three years in the hospital for treatment, he went on to become a journalist and editor. Mr. Henley was considered to have had a successful career, if for no other reason than his rousing influence on others due to his spirit and attitude.

The author of *Treasure Island*, Robert Louis Stevenson, was a friend of Henley's. He described Henley as "a great, glowing, massive-shouldered fellow with a big red beard and a crutch; jovial, astoundingly clever and with a laugh that rolled like music; he had an unimaginable fire and vitality; he swept one off one's feet." Stevenson wrote to Henley that his character Long John Silver had been inspired by Henley.

Nelson Mandela recited Henley's poem *Invictus* to other prisoners incarcerated alongside him. It was used in the Clint Eastwood film *Invictus* in 2009. In all likelihood his words have reached more people than he ever could have imagined, and his influence has altered lives for the better.

To know the words originated with a young boy who contracted tuberculosis, later lost his leg to amputation, and still found a way to have characteristics enviable enough to be represented in a classic book is amazing.

His will, drive, and upbeat attitude are a reminder to us all that though life may not always be fair we can do our utmost to respond to challenges in the best ways possible.

May you and your loved ones find the power to overcome life's setbacks and know that your influence on others, like Mr. Henley's, may go well beyond what you realize.

Choice Moments

If you have ever been frustrated by a situation you were stuck in, you are not alone. At times we get wrapped up in a difficult setting we would rather let pass us by. Unfortunately, in many of those instances, we don't have much control. Then we are tempted to contact friends and vent our complaints.

Pastor Pullin from a local retirement community, Greencroft, offered a thought in his Sunday class that really resonated with me. He said the Apostle Paul wrote his letter to the Philippians while he was imprisoned. Yet in the letter, Paul encouraged the Philippians to rejoice, regardless of circumstances.

Pastor Pullin highlighted the concept that we have a choice—to be grumblers, or to be grateful.

As he spoke to the group at Greencroft, I could only imagine how some of the people around him must be feeling. Many had given up their homes and life as they had known it, to prepare for the later years. The loss of so many components of their prior existence is probably overwhelming to many who move into retirement homes and communities. It is not a position many anticipated for their future.

Once in that position, though, Mr. Pullin reminded us—like the apostle Paul taught—there is a choice: to grumble, or to be grateful.

Though life frequently hands us situations we would rather not be in, we still make the decision as to whether we grumble. This is the behavior where we moan, complain, and let others know how heavy our load is. Some of us, myself included, seem to take great pleasure in this, acting as if there is some weird reward for our griping.

Unfortunately, this behavior blinds our ability to see all the good we have in our life and the many gifts we should be grateful for. The negativity mindset may also turn away those around us.

Going forward, if we find ourselves tempted to let loose on the perceived negatives we are experiencing, we might try a different route. Look at the polar opposite by asking ourselves, "What blessings and belongings do I have that I should be grateful for?" In most instances the good is so incredible, when we really stop to think about it, that we might change our whole mindset.

Looking at our life with eyes of gratitude helps us uplift ourselves as well as the family and friends we love. Being a grateful person also lets us be a shining light to everyone else around us, a light that can, instead of add darkness to others, be the warm brightness that helps scatter other people's darkness away.

May you discover all the good in your life and find the best in each situation that comes your way. And may you be an amazing brightness in the lives of others.

A Driver's Perspective

Many of us, including myself, allow ourselves to get irritated by things in life that aren't truly that big of a deal. The small nuances of other people, work, or social activities can build up until they seem to weigh us down.

Once while driving in heavy traffic on the way to a conference, I was cut off by a car rather abruptly. In my mind it was a rude gesture, as I was in a hurry and didn't want to be late. I carried the agitation with me all the way to my destination.

Rather than be grateful I had arrived on time and safe, I wouldn't let the agitation go. The incident had assumed a life of its own. I had to tell all who would listen over the next few hours.

In his book *Don't Sweat the Small Stuff, and It's All Small Stuff*, Richard Carlson reminds us how important it is to keep such events in perspective. When we keep our focus on what we need to be doing and we avoid trifles, we can maintain stronger relationships, lower blood pressure, and have a better outlook on our current circumstances.

Many troubles we encounter each day don't really have much bearing on our long-term future. It is our reaction to these incidents that lead to our own consequences.

The beauty of life is easier to see when we are in touch with the genuinely important facets of our existence. The commitment to keeping ourselves calm and steady allows us to handle more challenges. It is only with maturity and perspective that we can manage problems more effectively. If we "don't sweat the small stuff," we can learn to control our responses to inevitable problems that come. This, in and of itself, is one important way we can live a healthier and happier life.

May we each remember we cannot always control the circumstances of our day, but we can control our responses to the situations of the day. It is the mindset of keeping life's problems in perspective that gives us the power to be the best we can possibly be, for ourselves and for those around us.

Personal Victories

The wonders of people's lives always amaze me. Each person we meet has obstacles they have overcome, victories they've attained, and other life occurrences unique to them. It's magnificent to learn more about those we meet.

One gentleman, whom we had seen for a while in our office, shared that his family had owned a business in his former country. In his native land, he explained, the first-born son inherited the family business. The second son, which he was, did not inherit any component of the business, regardless of how hard he worked.

Due to the culture pushing against him as second son, and his family holding fast to the tradition, he chose to strike out on his own. With thirty dollars in his pocket, and not knowing English, he traveled by boat across the ocean to try making his way in America.

He found a job as a laborer in a manufacturing company and worked his way up to become a supervisor. After years of work, he was able to retire and enjoy the satisfaction of knowing he and his own family had done well.

In addition to celebrating fifty years of marriage, he and his wife are proud of their three children, who have served their communities as a policeman, a teacher, and a lawyer. His pleasant demeanor and good spirits shine brightly. The big decision to leave his homeland had opened doors that he and his children might never have known otherwise.

His story illustrates that we and those we meet each day have distinctive lives interwoven with our own challenges and victories, which have led us to where we are now. You are amazing in your own right, in your own form or fashion, as is everyone. The people we encounter each day are filled with incredible experiences.

Remember to reflect on the wonders of your past, and know that you are truly unique and special. Also take time more often to learn about those you encounter, and you might be amazed at what you discover.

A Eulogy to Remember

While reading the book *The Road to Character* by David Brooks, I paused to contemplate a point. The author discussed the difference between "resumé virtues" and "eulogy virtues." The former are the material- or achievement-centered components of life, while the latter are the values most would truly aspire to have.

Though many of us would like to live—and encourage our children to live—a life of the eulogy virtues, there is a strong tendency today to reward the resumé components of life. This means, in this time of technology and advancement, there is too much emphasis on the skills one accumulates, the resumé virtues.

The truth of who we are often lies in our core values, what others see in us each day and would say about us when thinking about who we really are. These, the eulogy virtues, include kindness, honesty, faithfulness, and value brought to relationships.

Most of us consider such features of our inner being as the more important virtues.

Even so, people spend stretches of their life focusing on the success of worldly accomplishments only to find they have passed by the value of relationships with loved ones.

Though most of us are guilty to some degree of misplaced priorities, it is worth reminding ourselves that who we are is ideally what we want others to say about us when we are gone (eulogy values). With this in mind, may we each take steps daily, even if the steps are small at first, toward becoming the person with the values we want remembered. It is through the culmination of these small steps that we build who we truly are as a person and positively affect the lives of others.

May you and those you care about find value in the actions you take each day to make the world around you a better place.

English Class

Throughout our lives countless people impact our life in some way. Whether it is someone who lifted us up, helped us through a bad time, or someone who threw roadblocks in our way, people influence our path. In the end, we ultimately need others for much of who we are and who we become.

In high school my English teacher for one year was Mrs. Mildred Porter. She was known for being a tough and strict teacher. She required excellence and your best effort to perform in her class. She was hard on grading and gave out very few A's.

Though I was a good student, I was not disciplined and dedicated enough to perform at the level she needed in her class. In fact, I got a C the first semester. For someone who was accustomed to getting A's and B's, this was crushing. In my mind I blamed her and her ways. There were many aspects of her grading, the volume of assignments, and the way she taught that made me feel her class was just not fair. My belief was that grade was her fault, not mine.

One of the things she instructed us to do was memorize a certain poem and share it by memory in front of the class. The poem was so long I wondered if it was possible, not to mention the sheer audacity she had to force us to say it in front of the class. But there was no way to avoid it, so I resolved to learn the poem like she asked. The poem was entitled "Don't Quit."

Though I didn't get an A in her class either semester, I learned more about composition and writing than I did in any other English course, before or after. Curiously, her disciplined and dedicated approach also showed me the right way to do my job.

As I think back now, her memory is one that holds strong in my mind as a mentor who shaped much of who I am today. Throughout my life I have also frequently called on the words of the poem "Don't Quit." The poem that I had felt at the time was something she forced on me has served as an inspiration through some of my most trying times.

As I have reached the age Mrs. Porter likely was when she taught me, I feel a true indebtedness for her taking the time to help me along in life. In fact, when I applied to medical school an essay was required. She was the person who helped turn those words I placed on paper with emotion into a true composition, one worth of being read by admissions counselors. She was someone special, and she helped me convey the passion I still feel today.

Know in life that the C we earn, the challenges we face, and the hills we must climb are part of what make us the strongest people we can be. When we take responsibility for who we are and where we are, we can learn from those who have been placed in our path.

At the same time, the people around us are an ongoing part of shaping who we are. The very people we feel are roadblocks might very well be the ones who help us when we need it most.

May we each find the good in the people around us every day.

Football Coach

A former Division I head football coach retired in Michiana to be near his grandchildren. In looking back at his career, he shared one of the memories that had made his occupation particularly worthwhile.

One of his college players had gotten into a fight and was arrested, and the coach drove to jail after midnight. Now, NCAA Division I rules prevented him from posting bail, but he was able to visit with the young man and make sure the right person was contacted to help him. The right person happened to be the boy's uncle, because at a young age the boy's mother had passed away and the father was not around anymore. So Coach waited for the uncle to post bail and helped get his young player home.

After the player completed his career at Washington State University, he was one of two team members on the defense who did not get an opportunity to continue playing football at the professional level. Coach sat with his now-former player and asked what he wanted to do. He answered that he wanted to do something with football but wasn't sure what. With a little help from Coach, he became a graduate assistant at a small college—coaching football.

Unfortunately, there he was at a bar, this time of legal age, and two of his friends got into a fight with some of the locals. Though he wasn't at fault, the fallout caused problems, so he again leaned on his old college coach.

The mentor believed the young man was good at heart. He gave him a supportive word for another position as a graduate assistant at the smaller Montana State University, explaining to the hiring university official that this young man was worth the risk.

Seasons passed without a great deal of communication between Coach and his former player, until the phone rang one night. Coach answered the phone to hear his former player's voice. He jokingly, but not sure of the response he would get, asked, "You're not in trouble with the law again, are you?"

The reply was reassuring. The former player said he was calling to let Coach know he had become a husband, father of two, and just received his Superbowl ring as the assistant receiver coach for the Green Bay Packers. He was calling to thank Coach for helping him become the upstanding father, husband, and assistant coach he had become. Without his love and support, he would not be where he was.

Coach shared his happiness with me that the young man who had no parents and all the reasons to give up had kept going.

Coach's willingness to lend a hand and his belief in the player had helped the young man to be and do things most people only dream of. Though most of us don't coach football players, we connect ourselves with people who need a hand up and an encouraging word. May we take Coach's example into our life and contribute a little time, caring, and mentoring to help make the world a better place, one person at a time.

Basketball Shoes

The power of a mentor can be incredible, regardless of age.

As an adult I can think of multiple people who helped mold and shape my career. As a child, the number is smaller, with my parents, grandparents, and an older brother leading the way.

Though I'm not quite sure why this memory came to mind, as a nine-year-old boy I wanted to wear my brother's old high-top canvas basketball shoes to watch a baseball game of his. Now mind you, he was seven years older, so his hand-me-down shoes really should have sat a few years before I put them on. But I was so proud to inherit the shoes he had recently outgrown, I simply had to wear them to his game.

One of the mothers in the baseball stands commented on my big shoes. I quickly pointed out that my toes had a ways to go to reach the end. Then I proudly shared how I secured a more solid fit by placing newspaper at the end of the shoes before putting them on.

It never dawned on me at that age to hold off wearing these oversized shoes. The truth was it made me feel big, like my older brother. Somehow the woman managed not to say anything, which would make me embarrassed about the situation.

It was not until I grew older that I realized the influence of my brother. He was someone I could look up to, emulate, and aspire to become. His example was one that set the bar high for me. Though he passed away in a car wreck at the age of seventeen, his integrity and work ethic are still talked about in my family today.

He was truly a mentor who took on the role in such a positive manner that he helped me strive to do right and be good—more than he ever knew. The significance of his mentorship carried on long after he was gone.

Though we each have mentors and those we have looked up to in our lives, we often forget the influence that we have on those around us. The way we handle ourselves, the honesty we share with others, and the integrity with which we live is on display to someone every day.

It is those around us who might very well use our actions as a guide. Though no one is perfect, reminding ourselves that our actions are on display more than we realize can help us set the best example for those who might be watching what we do.

You never know who might aspire to walk in your shoes.

Trains of the Thirties

The days of the past can be forgotten if someone does not write down what has happened. A small snippet of the life of a man who was ninety-nine when he came to the office highlighted this.

The kind gentleman was born in 1919. He shared that he loved bluegrass music, had been alive when former president Franklin Roosevelt passed away, and had spent time in the Navy. Then he said that his time in the Navy did have one small hiccup.

During a ten-day furlough, he came home to visit family. In those days he used the common serviceman method of transportation—hitchhiking from his naval base on the East Coast to Indiana. The time he spent with his family on their country farm was a much-needed reprieve from his service duties.

He had saved enough money to travel back to his base by train—the first time he would ever ride one. On the morning he walked to the rural train station, he was directed to an old, small building next to the tracks with no one in it. He waited patiently near it with ticket in hand. About the time he expected to get on, a big train blew past him. Bewildered by the occurrence, he waited on the platform. After waiting most of the day, he realized he was out of luck.

He got ahold of someone at the train company and told them what happened. They responded that it was his fault the train didn't stop. Flabbergasted, he asked what they meant.

The person told him, "There's a red lantern hanging at the end of the deck. When you see the train, you are to light it, wave it back and forth near the track, and then the engineer will stop the train."

"Now, how was a country boy like me, who has never been on a train, supposed to know that?" he asked.

The next day he followed the lantern instructions and was able to catch the train.

Unfortunately, he was a day late back to his duties. He was thrown into the brig, and then put on kitchen duty peeling potatoes.

He did mention to me, with eyes shining in good humor, that he'd met some very nice people on his penalty duties.

In hearing his story, I could not help but think about how many people have wonderful experiences that remind us who they were, where they have been, and what life was like in their time. I encourage you to jot down some of your present-day experiences and those of your family. The value may carry on much more than you can imagine for your family's future generations.

Where Closed Doors Lead

Hearing the retirement announcement of my former chairman of dermatology brought a flow of emotions to me. Mentors in life are not supposed to change, grow old, or retire. In fact, their memory is supposed to be held fixed in our mind just as it was years ago. At least, that was what my thoughts played out.

After coming to the realization that my mentor had actually made this choice, I needed to decide if we should shut down my practice to make the trip to his retirement gathering.

Oddly enough, it should not have been a decision at all. I am a bit like my former chairman in that I feel an obligation to be in the practice each day solving skin problems. Fortunately I have a wonderful bride who is often a better voice of reason. She said there was no way I would not be going, as this man and his team had provided us the opportunity to practice the specialty I love.

Upon arrival at the festivities, it was amazing to see all of the faculty, former residents, and others who had gathered to honor him. As a country bumpkin who feels fortunate to be doing what I do each day, I felt quite humbled to be in the room with these fantastic people.

Besides seeing my chairman/mentor and other familiar faces, one of the highlights came in the form of a memory shared. A prior resident reminded us that our chairman used to say—with a smile and excited expectancy before entering the next exam room—"You never know what is on the other side of that door!"

That thought has stood out to me during my career because it resonates with the way I feel each day. The people we care for are wonderful gifts and treasures. The personalities, their careers, hobbies, vacations, and so much more that people share with me every day make each day worthwhile.

Patients are so fascinating, they make each morning a joy to wake up for.

Each person is truly a gift. The dermatology conditions I treat are important, yet the human interaction with them is what I love. It makes each day magical.

The wonder of our life is not only in the job we do, it is also in the people we interact with. These moments with others can be opportunities for growth and endless new discoveries. The paths we cross have the power to uplift, inspire, and change the courses of lives—ours and theirs.

I encourage you to find the good in each person and to know that behind each door in life lies a wonderful person who is a treasure for that moment.

May you find the magic behind your next door.

About the Author

Dr. Roger T. Moore was raised in the small town of Elida (population 181), New Mexico, and later moved thirty miles to the big city of Portales (population 11,850). He grew up working on the family's farm and ranch, spending summers building fence, feeding and tending cattle, and driving tractors. Most summers he worked for his mother's father, Temple Rogers (who he was named after—Roger Temple Moore). His father often told young Roger that if he turned out like his grandfather he would be just fine. This grandfather was someone Roger always admired, looked up to, and emulated. Temple was regarded as the hardest working man in his town, an honest person of integrity, and a fellow who was a straight shooter.

Though neither of Roger's parents graduated college, each put incredible effort into him being able to reach his dreams. He feels he grew up as a most fortunate child because his mother, Annelle, and his father, Dick, made so much of his life possible.

Dr. Moore's initial passion in life was football, and he walked on at Texas Tech University for one year. After two surgeries on his knee, he returned home to the college in his hometown, Eastern New Mexico University. There he played linebacker for a conference champion team, until another knee surgery ended his playing career. The upbeat attitude and demeanor of his orthopedic surgeon, Dr. Bill Barnhill (a US Ski Team physician), inspired the recently injured Roger to become an orthopedic surgeon.

So Roger changed his major from marketing to pre-med his junior year of college, threw his heart into his studies, and set out to become a doctor. Changing areas of study so late in his college career required an inordinate amount of study. Dr. Moore attributes the work ethic his family instilled in him on the farm for giving him the wherewithal to make this change and climb the mountain of work ahead of him. The effort paid off—he gained entrance into four medical schools. He chose Texas Tech University Medical School, where he graduated near the top of his class, earning induction into the prestigious Alpha Omega Alpha honor society.

Entering his medical school training, Roger knew he loved surgery and the immediate results a patient received. Orthopedics was his desire. What he soon found out, though, was that he enjoyed getting to know patients and continuing his relationships with them even more. His heart was torn between following his mentor's path of orthopedics or finding an alternative career.

Fortunately and unfortunately, his father had squamous cell carcinoma of the lower lip before Roger entered medical school and had suggested dermatology as a career path. Roger researched this field and found that as a dermatologist he would perform procedures and surgeries, which gave him the satisfaction of cure and immediate results. At the same time, this area of medicine allowed him to maintain continuity of care with his patients, since many dermatology patients came in regularly for skin checkups. This would allow Dr. Moore to get to know his patients and continue caring for them over long periods of time. A perfect mesh was found.

Dr. Moore was able to gain entrance into the prestigious Rush-Presbyterian-St. Luke's Medical Center for his dermatology residency. There he worked with some of the iconic dermatologists of the modern era, including Dr. Arthur Rhodes (one of, if not the, leading mole guru of our time), Chairman Dr. Michael Tharp (an internationally recognized dermatologist for his work on hives and urticaria), Dr. Marianne O'Donoghue (an integral person in the American Academy of Dermatology who volunteered every Friday afternoon educating residents), and Dr. Mark Hoffman (one of the brightest minds in all of dermatology). Learning from these fine minds helped Dr. Moore attain the highest level of clinical skills in dermatology.

The passion Dr. Moore has for his specialty and his patients leads him to enjoy his work so much that he often tells his staff he feels like he is on vacation every day he works. At the same time, the primary joy of his job is the patients he is honored to care for each day. He feels humbled and appreciative of the opportunity to be a dermatologist. Dr. Moore states it is the patients, their lives, and their stories that inspire him every day to be the best he can possibly be.

Dr. Roger Moore is a board-certified dermatologist and the director and founder of the dermatology practice DermacenterMD, established in 2004. He provides a broad range of services, including skin cancer identification and treatment, Mohs micrographic surgery, general dermatology, and cosmetic rejuvenation through minimally invasive techniques. His patient following includes clients who travel from Michigan, Illinois, and Ohio, as well as Indiana to see him in Elkhart, Indiana.

A leader in skin cancer care and education, Dr. Moore has been a speaker at events in a vast geographic footprint extending from his home state of Indiana to Texas and California. He routinely teaches medical providers in his region as well as medical students through his role as the dermatology clerkship director at Indiana University Medical School in South Bend. He has also hosted nurse practitioners, physician assistants, and resident physicians for rotations through his clinic. He has contributed to research in medical dermatology and in cosmetic procedures, including botulinum toxin.

Dr. Moore founded and has been course director of Dermatology Summit, which educates and trains primary care physicians and non-dermatology providers, including nurse practitioners and physician assistants. He is also the innovator, founder, and president of Dermwise Inc., an online dermatology training platform used by dermatologists to help train their nurse practitioners and physician assistants. The Dermwise training has received endorsements from a variety of dermatology providers, most notably from Mayo Clinic graduate and past Illinois Dermatologic Society and Chicago Dermatologic Society past president Dr. Alix Charles. Dermwise has been used by dermatologists from California to West Virginia.

Dr. Moore knows the importance of continuing his own education. He maintains the highest level of continuing education, including courses from international leaders in cosmetic, medical, and surgical dermatology. He is a diplomate of the American Board of Dermatology, a fellow of the renowned American Academy of Dermatology, American Society of Dermatologic Surgery, American Society for Mohs Micrographic Surgery, and is a member of American Medical Association and Indiana State Medical Association. He takes very seriously his own knowledge and the trust his patients place in him as their provider.

He also enjoys writing his monthly newsletter, and small books like this one, to inform, entertain, and uplift his patients.

Dr. Moore knows every venture in life is not complete without family, and he is proud his wife has been the practice's administrator as well as his partner in life. He credits her for being the MVP, most valuable person, in the family and the practice. They have three children, a son and two daughters, who light up their lives.